GW01393113

Shhhh!!!! We Don't Talk About That
Taylor Crowshaw

Copyright © 2018 Taylor Crowshaw
Cover © 2018 Rob Croaker

All rights reserved. This book, or parts thereof, may not be reproduced or transmitted
in any form or by any means, electronic or mechanical, including recording,
photocopying, offset, or by any information storage and retrieval system without
permission in writing from the author, except by reviewers who may quote brief
passages to be printed in a magazine or newspaper.

ISBN: 978-1987474053

ACKNOWLEDGMENTS

Thank you to Rob and Jack who have encouraged me every step of the way. Without whose help, this book would never have seen the light of day.

Table of Contents

Introduction

My Gift

Part One: The Early Years

Introduction

You may not be interested in these words that I've invested.

But I just want you all to know this is our young life in rhyme.

One day you will understand how these words written by my hand.

Were done so you could pass down some history.

Instead of it being a mystery.

Now some of you may find this hard to read but hold your breath and please proceed.

Yes, there were times of strife.

It is all a part of life.

I am no different than many others with sisters and brothers.

Our story is here, for your eyes and ears.

Please enjoy and park your tears.

© 2018 Taylor Crowshaw

My Gift

I didn't write this book for money or glory.

Just for you and to tell my story.

Memories can be selective.

But they are mine, and I cannot be objective.

I hope you keep this close to your heart.

A gift from me my words impart.

One day when you are ready.

Keep your nerve and hold your pencil steady.

Dig deep down into your heart,

for your own secrets to impart.

It's not an easy thing to do, but

think of this poem and keep it true.

All our past makes us who we are.

Though we may never travel far.

Time is a precious gift so give your time

and make your list.

Leave your words for someone else, to

read and gain from their wealth.

© 2018 Taylor Crowshaw

Part One: The Early Years

The Beginning

I don't know very much about mum and dad's young lives.

I will lay down in words what I know.

To be honest the facts hurt me so.

At seven months my mother was born a tiny bundle all forlorn.

"She won't survive the night." is what they

said, as they laid her on the bed.

A precious bundle in a shoe box.

Left beside the fireside.

A special lady saw a future for her.

She would not let her granddaughter die.

Gently she tended her.

Fed her milk with a glass eye dropper.

Nowadays that would be improper.

No Special Care or incubator.

Just leave her be and check her later.

She fought all night for her life.

A stronger woman I never knew.

All of her life that remained true.

My mother.

A tired and heavily pregnant lady on the sofa lay.

Needing to sit and rest for part of the day.

A young neighbour took her toddler for a walk.

Up the road and to the pond.

I am not sure exactly what went wrong.

In that pond little Freddie drowned.

The lady when told went into shock.

Off into her bedroom the door to lock.

A few weeks later my father was born.

The lady couldn't look at him or even kiss or cuddle him.

To her bedroom she would go.

Still shocked and feeling such sorrow.

Maybe she would get better.

Hopefully... some tomorrow.

As a child he didn't talk but he still learned how to walk.

He was not to blame for this tragedy.

Still it was such a shame.

Lives shattered by an accident.

Nothing would ever be the same.

As he grew he learned to talk, just

as he had learned to walk.

That poor lady was my grandmother,

and the boy my father.

© 2018 Taylor Crowshaw

Our Backyard

The sun shone bright in our back yard.

The air was light in our back yard.

A picnic blanket on the floor.

Mum's latest book open waiting.

The smell of Ambre Solaire and mum's skin baking.

It was a castle or a shop.

A sheet hung across the line.

We'd put on a show and fill our time.

I had pet spiders on the gate, Fred and Henry were my mates.

It rained a lot in our back yard.

Cold and wet in our back yard.

All of those things I didn't mind.

It had a mystery of a kind.

Dreams were dreamt, and plans were made.

A maiden to rescue and dragon to be slayed.

No technology to steal our time.

Just imagination and a washing line.

Our back yard was very small.

Just a fence and a couple of walls.

It provided us with space to grow.

Before off into the world we'd go.

© 2018 Taylor Crowshaw

The Backstreet

Out in our backstreet that is where our friends would meet.

We'd play marbles in the grid, and on the ice, we would skid.

String thread through old tin cans, one day a phone the next day stilts.

American and French skipping.

Twigs for imaginary horses whipping.

Next door but two there lived a family of four.

I remember they had a big black door.

On occasion we would be let in as long as we did not make a din.

It was a different world to our back yard.

More like a picture on a greetings card.

Flowers blossomed in abundance.

A neat clipped lawn on either side of a concrete path two feet wide.

On the top of their garage was a large black tank.

When the weather was hot it became a paddling pool.

In which we all kept cool.

Sometimes if we were lucky and hung around not looking too mucky.

"Come on in." we'd be invited.

In we would march determined and united.

After a while when the fun was all over.

We would be sent back outside.

Into our backstreet, all our other friends to greet.

There, we would play all day.

Maybe popping in for dinner.

Quickly trying to get away.

Mum would lean out of the window "Come on in its time for bed."

With our final goodbyes over and plans made to meet up tomorrow.

Off inside we would head.

© 2018 Taylor Crowshaw

My Dad Worked at the ICI

My dad worked at the ICI our bins were only three feet high.

Not full of rubbish to the sky.

Trousers tucked into his socks off he goes on his bike.

Head down against the wind, he took flight.

We timed him home, whilst we stood at the garden gate.

To see him in the distance flying.

To beat his homeward record, trying.

"Well kids did I do it?" "Nearly dad." We'd say.

"There goes another one, he worked in Plastics same age as me I'll be next, just you see." He says as he wades his way through the obituaries.

My dad worked at the ICI

Sometimes he'd be brought home bent double.

When his back was giving trouble.

We would always know the score.

A couple of days on the bedroom floor.

Sundays he was on a mission.

The usual, he'd gone fishing.

White hankie out of the window his signal home.

No such thing as a mobile phone.

My dad worked at the ICI

Thursdays payday chippy dinners and the Christmas parties were always a winner.

He always called those he didn't know.

Either, Jack....or.... Joe.

My dad worked at the ICI

Grandad and uncles on both sides braved the elements and high tides.

I asked him one day, "Would you not go?"

In surprise he turned to me, and looked at me, he was not messing.

He then spat out as if confessing.

"Go to sea? No no love. That's not the life for me."

My dad worked at the ICI

Dedicated to my father.

© 2018 Taylor Crowshaw

I Am an Orphan Now (Age 46)

I used to rise from my bed.

I'd hit mum with a slipper on her head.

Just to make sure she wasn't dead.

Such was the fear I had as a child.

I used to dream she'd been replaced, by an alien from outer space.

That she wore a mask.

Which she would take off, if I was brave enough to ask.

Such was the fear I had as a child.

I dreamt she was inside a box.

She couldn't get out it was locked.

I sobbed so loudly she would awake.

I'd feel her gently stroking my brow and she would whisper softly.

"Hush hush now."

She was the one to who I could cry, and she would know the reason why.

When she died I howled like a wolf who was alone.

Calling all his family home.

"Mum. I am an orphan now."

© 2018 Taylor Crowshaw

Our Poodle

One day mum went to the local shop we thought to buy a bottle of pop.

Instead she brought home a toy poodle.

What should we call him?

Perhaps Noodles.

Small and white with curly fur you could hardly see that he was there.

He even had a pedigree, Champagne Charlie that was he.

He would walk around the block, every day off he would trot.

One day while out on his lap he never did make it back.

Later on, there came a knock at the door.

After 13 years, he was no more.

© 2018 Taylor Crowshaw

Uncle Harold

My dad met him one windy day across the rezy when he was fishing.

He was so dapper in his clothes.

Sporting a pencil moustache, under his nose.

They grew to be good friends and uncle to us he became.

In those days the friends you knew were usually uncle and aunty too.

He would come for Sunday dinner and when he did we were on a winner.

He bought me a fury gonk and my sister too.

Hers was a deep red, and mine was turquoise blue.

Such exotic creatures you'd wash their coats and brush their hair.

His sister gave me my first job, I'd work all weekend for ten bob.

Stacking towels and washing hair sweeping the floor and making tea.

It was just the thing for me.

Enids at the top of town.

Another good shop, long closed down.

Uncle Harold was one of those, who took great pride in his clothes.

He was a gentleman in both senses of the word.

He was a very decent man, who really cared.

© 2018 Taylor Crowshaw

Bonfire Night

Now behind our house on a triangle of land each family built a bonfire with their own hands.

There was a big one in the middle.

To the Heathie mob it did belong, but please correct me if I'm wrong

Now my mum she was a lady graceful and elegant.

She smelled of perfume lipstick and cigarettes.

She once got into The Bluebells dancing troupe.

My nanna would not let her go

She needed her it was just so.

Now she wasn't spoiling for a fight when she went out on that night

Usually all is fine, but there was a glitch this time.

There came a gang around the fire.

I don't think they that they were local, but soon they became quite vocal.

Mum went out to stop their antics.

We watched on from the bedroom window frantic.

Mum in curlers all alone in the middle of the gang.

As we did sit, and tremble mother was magnificent.

A teenage girl lunged for her, but mother took her by the hair.

She slung her around and threw her down.

"Don't you come around here again" I could hear her shout,

"Off with you, you're nothing but a group of louts".

So, she dusted off her hands, and left them all behind.

Head held aloft she marched back home.

That was the mother that I remember fierce and proud with a bit of a temper.

Now, there are a few things before I go that I think you all should know.

As the excitement it was mounting and the minutes we were counting.

"You'll have to wait until it's dark." My mum and dad would bark.

It was the best bonfire night.

Watching those fireworks take flight.

Catherine Wheels, toffee apples, and treacle toffee.

Baking potatoes in the fire, while watching those rockets zooming higher.

As the embers they died down, we head back in with a frown.

Our smutty faces washed and red.

Off we shuffled to our bed.

© 2018 Taylor Crowshaw

The Lakes

We went camping there one year we took our dog and all our gear.

Our dad sat fishing by the lake.

We stayed at the campsite breakfast to make.

There was much excitement there.

We'd scoop the leaves and throw them up, to have them landing in our hair.

The water softly lapped the shore the sun was shining bright.

The fishes they were leaping, much to our delight.

Later on, that day my sister, she went missing.

You guessed it my dad and brother they were fishing.

My mum was frantic with worry, she ran everywhere in a great hurry.

Up and down the hilly lanes in the ditches and the drains.

We searched for her in despair.

Hand in hand I can remember that we ran and ran.

The sound of an engine, rumbles along behind us.

A man rolls down his window, "Have you lost a child?"

Mother's eyes shine brightly with tears as this strange man allays her fears.

"I took her to the local town, jump right in I'll take you down."

When they were united mother got quite cross and took her back to the lake to see the boss.

Our father then decided that we should go straight home.

"Never again." They swore would she be left alone.

© 2018 Taylor Crowshaw

Our Old Wardrobe

There once was a wardrobe standing tall in our room.

I can even see it now in the morning gloom.

With frost on the window panes we would wake up each winters day.

I'd try and swap my side of the bed, I'd wet it once again.

I thought, that I could blame my sister as a child.

It's only now that I realise those fantasies were wild.

The springs poked through the mattress horse hair popping out.

As we rolled into the middle we would scream and shout.

Mum would say, "Be quiet you two, or I'll be in there in a minute."

My sister would laugh, and I would beg, "Please don't you drop us in it."

Next door but one there lived a lady Mrs. Fenton she was called.

Her husband worked in the engine sheds, just across the road.

She would sit, day after day at her sewing table.

Making fancy clothes for that she was quite able.

Sometimes she would make us, what we called a frock.

I can hear your laughter.

Now there is no need to mock.

Do you remember at the beginning of this tale?

I mentioned our old wardrobe, but to what avail?

Well if you had opened the door nice and wide.

You would have seen two dresses hanging side by side.

Two small dresses and two small pairs of shoes was all that was inside.

Please do not feel pity that we had no clothes to wear.

We had our mum and our dad, and a worn-out teddy bear.

© 2018 Taylor Crowshaw

Granny and Grandad

As a child I didn't know that granny and grandad loved me so.

That when my sister she was born they didn't want me to go home.

I had an accident there one day, cut my lip just a tip, but my mum she was furious.

I was just a child and probably got curious.

We visited once a week although they did not live far.

Those were in the days before we had a car.

They had colour TV and sat there watching cricket.

We looked on in awe as the umpire shouted, "Wicket."

We jostled for the little stool which they brought out and we thought cool.

Granny in her rollers, jowels hanging down.

She was really kindly, but always wore a frown.

Grandad was small in stature never saying much.

He would make us a drink of pop such a lovely treat.

We only ever had at home the Corporation kind, but we didn't mind.

One day I saw my dad clutching a letter.

I had seen him looking better.

Granny she died that day, I think it was her heart.

I had never ever seen granny and grandad apart.

Every Tuesday evening my dad would go and visit.

Just for a couple of hours.

Striding on his long legs to see his father and to share the news

I think they had very similar views.

Years went by in this routine.

Before grandad started to get frail.

As dad and his brother sat beside his bed, he began to fail.

It wasn't very long just a week or two before he joined my granny and then they were as one.

© 2018 Taylor Crowshaw

I Can Swim

I learnt to swim in the sea with my mother holding me.

Around and round my arms would flap, with her holding onto my back.

I'd crawl along in the paddling pool.

Thinking I was really cool.

As I got a little older, and the water began to feel much colder.

She would let go of my back.

I could swim and that was that.

© 2018 Taylor Crowshaw

We Went to The Baths Today

"Mum can we go to the baths today?"

"To the baths, no." She'd say.

She would shout, "It's raining." and in response we would plead, "But mum we're in training."

She would sigh and say no, but in the end, she would let us go.

Off we went for the day to the baths to swim and to play.

We were only nine or ten way back then.

In those days there was less danger and most children were free rangers.

Tuppence clasped in sweaty palms.

Threadbare towels tucked under arms.

We'd pay our fee and get a ticket push through turnstiles, we were in, squealing, "Let the fun begin."

Dark and cold changing room.

We never did mind the gloom.

Walking around the balcony looking for friends, staring out to sea.

Jumping in at the deep end and looking up in wonder.

"Should we? Would we climb up to the top board, and jump in?" I thundered.

Not for me those scary boards and diving.

I could swim like a fish and was positively thriving.

Scrambling up onto the fountain you would have imagined, it was the highest mountain.

When lightning struck we were all called out.

Then back in with a shout

On our way home just for a treat.

It was time to get something nice to eat.

Rimmers lollies or parched peas, I loved the both of these.

"What a day." We would yawn as we fell asleep.

"Same again tomorrow?"

"You bet," we agreed, "and we will take a mighty feed."

© 2018 Taylor Crowshaw

Shhhh!!!! We Don't Talk About That

Now you have to remember these are in the days of old when the worst you had was a cold.

Before mental health existed.

No such thing as being ill....in the mind....it was a bitter pill.

Shhhh!!!! We don't talk about that

Twelve, seven, and six we were, when first mum threw her hands up in despair.

No more stories in their bed or staying up past mum's watershed.

Grandparents in denial, "It must be you you're such a trial," and a vague memory of a bible.

Whispered secrets in the dead of night.

Things children shouldn't hear.

Memories still vivid and clear.

A man in a suit with a briefcase a doctor too, "You need to sign this." He said to mum, and then they were gone.

One brief visit to Ridge Lee I think we had a cup of tea.

We got home from school one day to find him splayed upon the floor.

We jumped onto his lap in delight.

We thought he was back, but he'd taken flight.

Escaped for the day to come home and then he was gone.

No such thing as counselling, talking things through.

Just electric shocks and medication, "You'll get over it, get on with it old son."

He came home to bed and rested there the longest time.

He was our dad, yes and he was fine.

Time passed by and he got better.

He went back to work and took a letter.

"The only job that you can do is cleaning up and making a brew."

He did this job with pride, but on that day something inside him died.

We don't talk about that....

© 2018 Taylor Crowshaw

The Reservoir

When we lived on Radcliffe Road in those days of old.

Before there was any Copse Road.

There once was a reservoir.

We could see it from afar.

No access in those days on a bike.

You crossed the trams and then the dyke.

Dad would go fishing there.

Running his fingers through his thick black hair.

Staring into the murky deep.

For those fishes he would seek.

Sat upon those sloping cobbles.

Waiting patiently for his float to wobble.

There it goes, his hands a tremble, reel him in, nice and gentle.

We would go sometimes and sit with him.

Silently waiting in anticipation of this giant in the deep.

Who generally slumbered fast asleep.

"Can we go home dad were bored?"

He nodded silently and off we strode.

We only lived across the road.

One day my sister she went a crashing into the brambles and got a lashing.

My dad did sigh in relief.

Due to the fact that his daughter, did not end up in the water.

My brother he would go there too.

Just like his father through and through.

Faces rapt in concentration keep nets ready at their station.

Friday night was competition this is when they would do their wishing.

"Let it be, my turn tonight, don't let the fishes all take flight."

At the weigh in they were anxious.

To see those nets with fish a thrashing.

After all.

It was their passion.

© 2018 Taylor Crowshaw

A Tale of Two Men

One of them you'd feel pity for and the other you would kick out the door.

Now this was in the summer when mum's underwear went missing.

My father, he was always going fishing.

They lay in bed one summers' eve and got a sense of tension.

It was a while before one of them even gave it a mention.

A soft thud and footsteps as down his ladder a man descended.

My father he jumped up his home to be defended.

"He must have been looking in." My father said his face was grim.

Now you may think this story has the makings of a farce.

All my dad wanted to do was kick him up the arse.

The next day, he lay in wait for him to open up the gate.

As he lifted aloft his ladder my dad he began to get madder.

Mum knocked on the window pane it gave him such a fright.

He picked up his ladder and took off home that night.

Dad followed him back home.

Then ran quickly to the telephone.

We never heard any more, and mum's underwear stayed on the line.

Unlike before.

The other half of this tale is quite short, but nevertheless is of import.

Please continue to pay attention as I give this poor chap a mention.

Sometime in the winter with cold everywhere.

Under our old porch slept a man, of whom we were not aware.

Until one day our dad came home and woke his fitful slumber.

He told that young man there and then then to do a number.

I often think of that young man for I do not think that he was old.

Did he get a helping hand, and come in from out the cold?

© 2018 Taylor Crowshaw

The Accident

One fine day just for a lark.

My brother rode off to the Memorial Park.

Later, on the pier they played prize bingo.

It was surely worth a go.

They won a pile of tickets but whose they were.

How would they share?

This they did not know.

His friend and he got into a tussle but unfortunately, he didn't have much muscle.

He hit his face upon a rock and wandered home half in shock.

He went to bed that night, even though he'd had a fright.

When he woke up in agony his face loose.

Jawline all askew.

What should my mother do?

"We'll whip him up to Blackpool Vic. Yes" she said "That will do the trick."

A few days passed, and he came home.

His mouth a mass of wire.

He huddled up in a chair right beside the fire.

A straw was his new spoon as he sucked up his soup day after day.

He hasn't touched a drop since needless to say.

Six weeks went by in slow motion.

Would he look ok?

We didn't have a notion.

The big day came to unzip him.

He was dressed quite formal.

When we saw him later on he almost looked normal.

Just let me make it very clear.

He was very normal in those days.......other than his ears.

For my brother...

© 2018 Taylor Crowshaw

Our Teenage Years

In those years it was our passion to be the height of fashion.

It may surprise our kids that in that era we had fashion, it couldn't be clearer.

Those were the days when you cross the road to avoid your parents.

Not much has changed in that direction, but we can look back with affection.

We would rock up to the pier.

Wearing all our latest gear.

It all started with flared hipster trousers and shiny blouses.

Hot pants and miniskirts.

Wait a minute I'm trying to remember.

Crombie coats and Doc Martens never fear I'm only just starting.

Oxford Bags and Harrington jackets Ben Sherman shirts that cost a packet.

When T Rex Rode a White Swan.

Barry White, Mott The Hoople and The Who, I could go on.

I once had a friend with a Prince of Wales check coat.

I could only look in envy.

You know just who you are...... your father had a Jaguar.

Two-tone suits and fluffy jackets.

Music loud what a racket.

Moving on a few short years.

Frilly shirts and Tears for Fears,

Adam Ant and Ian Drury.

He played those drums in a fury.

David Bowie, and Rod Stewart but for me they didn't do it.

New Romance was my bag, I know most men found it a drag.

I hope I haven't bored you stiff, it wasn't my intention, but I thought that the fashions then.

Deserved a little mention.

© 2018 Taylor Crowshaw

I'm Still Crying

My mother wept beside my bed.

Resting her hand upon my head, "Just fourteen, just fourteen, all of your life ahead."

My dad wanted me to carry on, "Teach her a lesson." Is what he said.

Mum just could not get it into her head.

To Liverpool on the bus we went just the three of us.

"Just in time." Said the doctor as he laid me upon the bed.

They wheeled me off there and then.

"Please mum, please mum." I said.

I woke up in a mess.

In a room on my own.

Matron strode in looking on stern and tense. "That's what you get for messing."

I'm still crying now.

The next day as we travelled home on that bus all forlorn.

I rested my head on my father's shoulder and cried.

I don't know if I saw a tear in his eye it wasn't clear.

My abiding memory of that day is a butterfly that I set free.

He flew far away from me.

Girls would shout murderer as I walked along.

That was very, very wrong.

We both cried through the school railings.

He got me a teddy but that didn't change things.

Eventually we got married, but shortly after I miscarried.

His mother said, "It's just a day job son don't worry she'll be fine."

I'm still crying.

I am not trying to patronise.

Just to open up your eyes.

It's not just the young that I'm addressing when telling you to quit your messing.

If all you want is to have some fun, then please don't use a loaded gun.

Let this poem be a lesson to all of those to quit their messing.

They don't know the damage they do.

This much, I know is true.

I'm not ashamed I don't look back.

I was a child, but it changed me.

If I could I would alter time and try to rearrange it.

Having another family, will not even set you free.

You can never change it.

Over forty years have gone, and I'm still crying for my little ones...

© 2018 Taylor Crowshaw

The Darkness

Now there is something I must confess.

That I really should address.

A darker side to the story of our young lives.

My father he was charming and could be quite disarming.

His drinking pals thought him witty.

Sometimes his actions were not pretty.

They never realised that the drinks he bought took the food from our mouths.

Mother never had much of a life.

Whilst coping with all the strife.

Fridays he would go to The Legion up the road.

Drinking and gambling until the early hours.

Rolling home then falling through the door.

Landing in a messy heap on the floor.

Before we went on holiday.

He gambled all the money away.

A day out in the Isle of Man.

Money lost the night before.

Mother shouted as she slammed the door.

Nothing for a treat, just a packet of custard creams to eat.

He would not always take his pills, and that would sometimes make him ill.

He suffered from schizophrenia,

Not aggressive just depressive.

We walked on eggshells in the house.

Making hardly any noise, just like a mouse.

She kept the family afloat paid the mortgage and bought food.

The money he gave her paid a couple of bills.

My mother always wore a shell it made her hard but kept her well.

She gave him a normal life but paid for that with her own life.

Now please do not get me wrong I am not complaining, it was our life it is a fact.

I loved them both with all my heart.

Of our lives this is only a part.

Sometimes on a Friday when he came home, he would bring me something nice to eat.

We would sit up chatting for hours, with me sat by his feet.

So, you see it was not all bad.

Just sometimes a little sad.

They both gave us different gifts, to take with us on our journey of life.

I think of them with tenderness and deep affection.

My mother was quite a woman and my dad a unique kind of a man.

They were like the rest of us flawed but doing all we can.

As the years rolled on, and dad's vices were all gone.

He remembered to take his pills

Hardly ever getting ill.

My dad always maintained his wit

We laughed with him quite a bit.

Life had a simple pattern.

Nothing very much did happen.

Until my family moved away, but that is a tale for another day.

© 2018 Taylor Crowshaw

My First Proper Job

I had worked from the age of twelve.

Enids at the top of town, The Chinese Restaurant, The Steakhouse, The Mount Hotel, Woolies
and the Pier.

Had I not gone out to work.

There would have been no school shirt.

No school bag.

Just a bunch of rags.

When I left school in seventy-five.

A secretarial course completed.

There was no shortage of work.

Never any excuse to shirk.

My first proper job.

Where I earned more than a few bob.

A junior receptionist at a solicitor's office.

I thought that I would answer the phone.

Make tea and file documents away.

However, what I didn't realise.

Was that the senior partner had other ideas.

He wanted to use my shorthand and typing skills.

For typing letters and drafting wills.

He was an imposing character.

He would lean over me whilst he dictated.

With his fat cigar billowing smoke.

I would try to concentrate and not to choke.

Now I was only a young girl of sixteen.

Looking for knowledge to glean.

Anxious to get things right.

Higher things in my sights.

I was also told that he could read shorthand himself.

Well can you imagine how I felt.

I would take down his dictation some words were new to me.

Often when we'd finished he would request a cup of tea.

Usually it would be correct, but on the odd occasion.

I would have to refer to him and ask what he had said.

All a tremble I would approach his office and knock upon the door.

He would shout, "Enter." and I would proceed across the floor.

"Read it back to me." He would say.

This I would do and then be sent away.

I didn't always get an answer.

He would tell me to use my common sense.

To a girl of sixteen the responsibility was immense.

When I presented the work to be signed.

It usually worked out and everything was fine.

That solicitor later on became a Judge.

He taught me to have confidence in myself.

Thank goodness technology moved on.

Dictaphones, and electric typewriters.

Word processors and now computers.

The strange fact is.

I find myself every now and then.

Writing in shorthand as I hold my pen.

© 2018 Taylor Crowshaw

Part Two: Three Weddings and Ten Children

The End of Youth

The car glided with me inside it.

Wedding dress and flowers clutched in shaking hands.

"It's not too late." Dad said to me. "We can turn around and go for tea."

Wise words from a man I loved.

I thought I knew it all back then.

That would not happen and won't until who knows when.

We married just to prove them wrong.

Throwing our lives away for a song.

A few months in I realised I had seen him through misty eyes.

A marriage doomed from the start.

We soon began to drift apart.

I left one cold winters morn.

His heart lay broken hurt and torn.

You cannot stay out of pity or guilt.

Marriage on solid ground should be built.

What I didn't know that day.

Was that a child inside me lay.

A few months on when my son was born.

My life began, and my youth was gone.

© 2018 Taylor Crowshaw

I Have Had A Life

A new life stirs within me. A small foot making me aware of his existence.

I wait for his fathers return from work.

A favourite meal cooked and ready.

Eyes on the time. I wonder, where is he?

When I have cooked a special tea.

A strange feeling weighing heavy.

A knock at the door.

Keep it steady.

A greeting with arms outstretched.

Something was wrong I had guessed.

Walking slowly to the car we didn't have to travel far.

Drs. faces whispered phrases.

Numbness spreading to my heart.

Would he make it?

No one knew.

There wasn't much anyone could do.

Time would tell just how bad it would be.

We all had to wait and see.

Scans and tests completed.

The Dr. said, "Please be seated.

His brain is damaged beyond repair, he will never be the same.

He will not be the man you knew.

He may even dislike you."

All of this and more was true.

I didn't know just what to do.

We tried so hard to get help.

He didn't want to hurt me.

So, he set me free to live my life.

He didn't want me as his wife.

It wasn't easy even then, but time moved on.

Children to be raised and kept in mind.

Still he was not very kind.

After all these years, and a river of salty tears,

I do not feel bitter, sad, or sorry.

All of that has gone.

You see I have had a life, and he has had none...

© 2018 Taylor Crowshaw

The One

He was the one...yes, the very one.

Here it is some information.

So please be seated at your station.

I wasn't looking for a man or even a companion.

Just a dance and some fun.

From emotion at that time I'd run.

Around the gallery we would walk.

Sometimes we would stop to talk.

Giggling girls a little tipsy.

Nearly time to go home.

One last dance or maybe not.

I saw a man approaching us.

He was quite cute in his half a suit.

First one and then another, "Do you want a dance?" He would ask.

The girls all wore a sullen mask.

He took me out onto the floor.

As I leaned into his arms I succumbed

to his charms.

That night I knew he would mine for life.

Two years later I became his wife.

Many years on I feel the same as the day I took his name.

I never believed in love at first sight, but it happened to me on that night.

My beloved Peter.

© 2018 Taylor Crowshaw

When Peter Met Barbara

One snowy Christmas it was time to present my new man.

My brother had a party that year.

Full of good food and good cheer.

As I knocked on the door.

Inside my mother lay upon the floor.

Legs spread wide and loudly grunting.

I could only stare at the Christmas bunting.

They were playing charades under the Christmas tree.

Yes, you guessed it.

She was acting out the movie Born Free.

My mother was quite a character.

She thought me a bit uptight.

I certainly was on that night.

Peter had a lot of fun as he drank his beer and gazed on.

Barbara welcomed him warmly as she

rose from the floor.

He waved a greeting to all from the door.

I was surprised on that night that he never did take flight.

We look back now with fondness at all of my mother's nonsense.

A lady is what she always was.

Except when playing cards or perhaps...charades.

© 2018 Taylor Crowshaw

For You Too

This is a poem of many words.

Some of which you have already heard.

The day you came into my life all

hair and beauty, I recall.

You were only very small.

Your heart is huge you always care.

You are so precious still.

I love you now and always will.

You came to me in quite a hurry, causing

me a little worry.

Two weeks on you became very ill.

It was a while before your booties you could fill.

Now you've grown into a man.

You do all that you can.

I love you with all my heart.

Though we live hundreds of miles apart.

A little angel when you were born.

Quiet and thoughtful with a crown of golden hair.

We could take you anywhere.

A caring nature is you're gift.

You give our weary hearts a lift.

Thank you for being there. We love you darling so please take care.

This little girl was not in a hurry,

All of the day and half the night.

My body did not give up the fight.

As a child you were so organised,

In the wardrobe stacking clothes.

You were only two years old.

Deep in thought you often were.

Not like a child who doesn't have a care.

My heart swells each time I look at you.

So full of love this is true.

When I carried you I was in pain.

It was such a relief when you came.

Such a happy beautiful child, although you could be quite wild.

I always did enjoy our talks.

Whilst we were out on our walks.

The love we feel is hard to bear.

Our love for you is beyond compare.

You were always so laid back.

Even in the womb you lay back to back.

Staring around taking everything in.

Never once making a din.

A beautiful face and silky hair.

Thoughtful and considered you always were.

You used to hide when you got tired.

Off to bed before the dark.

Our love for you we cannot hide for eternity it will abide.

A little dot when you were born.

We were alone when you entered the world.

Just me and my little girl.

Your eyes were a crystal blue.

I loved the exotic look of you.

From early on you could walk and talk. A fashionista as a woman and a child.

By nature, calm and caring.

You never did mind sharing.

We Love you beyond measure.

To us you are a treasure.

Well what can I say.

You didn't arrive into this world easily that day.

You kicked and busted your way out.

You gave a wail and then a shout.

Always impatient to make a start.

Independent and quite smart.

You had a great big smile.

melting our hearts all the while.

You are always bright and breezy.

Loving you is very easy.

I remember the day you were born.

Staring out of the window waiting for your father to arrive.

Excitement mounting waiting for you to appear.

You were a beauty, smiling from ear to ear.

You bring such joy to our lives.

Full of fun and the odd surprise.

A beautiful woman you became.

Our deep love for you remains the same.

A late present is what you were.

A gift that we appreciate even although your arrival was late.

You always have a smile and lots of chat.

Great company and interesting.

Even though the intensity can be testing.

We are thankful for you every day.

In so many different ways.

You fill our lives with life and light.

Giving us the strength to go on and fight.

Loving you is easy too.

So, my darling we thank you.

This poem is for all of you, and my little ones who I never knew.

For my wonderful children.

© 2018 Taylor Crowshaw

For You My Son

The days are long for you my son.

Things go wrong for you my son.

Life is tough for you my son.

Emotions are oceans for you my son.

Your children are precious to you my son.

Your life is lived for them my son.

Trying to do it all for them my son.

Nothing left for you my son.

You have to listen to me my son.

If you're not here for them my son.

Who is going to care like you my son.

You have a duty of care my son.

That duty of care IS TO YOU.

MY SON

© 2018 Taylor Crowshaw

Anybody's Story

Your smile sits like a frozen mask.

An 'I'm ok' ready should anybody ask.

Sorrow hidden behind a fragile screen,

always felt but never seen.

You can strangle the fear with the written

word, and finally let your voice be heard.

The past follows in the shadows.

Always waiting to be announced.

It belongs to you.

Cast it off and be done.

You know this battle can be won.

© 2018 Taylor Crowshaw

Part Three: A New Start

A New Start

Piled into an old Audi A6 we packed up our home and picked up sticks.

A 30-foot removal van with two helpers and one main man.

We drove off to the ferry that day to make a new life and lessen the strife.

I left behind a precious son he had a job and would not come.

The sea was rough and so were we.

Bodies lay everywhere groaning loudly in despair.

When we landed on that night the weather was an awful sight.

We drove on for a couple of hours.

No Google maps or sat nav.

Just directions written down.

Which way to head from the nearest town.

When made it to our friends that night,

we were in for an awful fright.

The house we were supposed to rent had been sold, we would have to go.

It was a pity that we did not know.

The next day with the van unpacked.

Beautiful furniture piled into two old sheds.

We finally made it to our beds.

Within 10 days we had moved again.

Packed up our family and our things.

Travelled over a hundred miles.

With children no longer full of smiles.

We rented an old derelict farmhouse.

Whilst renovating our own old house.

This is the beginning of another part of my life.

As a mother a labourer and a wife.

© 2018 Taylor Crowshaw

No Baby

When we landed I began to feel quite sick.

Weeks we all spent feeling sick and ill.

We had no water at the time.

Just from a stainless-steel tank which the farmer had supplied.

The pigs from the piggery next door, had drunk the well dry.

I went for my first anti natal appointment.

There they told me my baby had died.

It wasn't like at home.

You would have it all over in a day, and the pain would go away.

It was procedure here to let nature take its course.

Nature stubbornly decided it wasn't going down that road.

My body wanted to carry on.

Even though the baby's life had gone.

Day after day feeling worse.

The weeks went by and nothing occurred.

I just had to see a doctor and to have my voice heard.

A kind doctor decided to take me in.

It wasn't easy you can imagine.

No point in discussing the nitty gritty.

It was just sad and a great pity.

After a while it was all over, and I could grieve and get on with life.

As I have said many times before.

As any woman will understand.

I still grieve for my lost little ones

© 2018 Taylor Crowshaw

A Shock

When we moved here it was a shock to

realise that we were mocked.

We thought of the Irish as a gentle friendly race.

Not only to our face.

What lay behind those smiles became

apparent to our child.

When going to school on the bus an

egg thrown into her face.

Go home you Brits they shouted, and

many other insults were touted.

We were never taught the history at school.

Unlike those children on that bus who

were taught relentlessly to hate us.

Not directly with spoken words, but

with the history that they heard.

The cruelty of the British during the famine, most British people never knew.

The desperate acts during the troubles on both sides to us was something new.

It is over 20 years ago but still the thought gives me a chill.

It's nothing personal we were told.

We were accepted and treated well.

Although work was hard to find.

In general people were kind.

It gave me a taste of how long ago our friends were treated when off they would go.

To build the British roads, railways and underground

No friendliness for them to be found.

Such prejudice and hate is very hard to equate.

This beautiful island is our home.

It is where our children and grandchildren

have grown.

Grandchildren of mixed decent diluting

the hatred that was felt.

Giving hope for a future of equality for all.

Prejudice is not determined by the colour of our skin.

It is fermented within our homes, our schools, our friends.

And in those places, it needs to end.

© 2018 Taylor Crowshaw

The Race

A corrugated piece of tin covers the tank

our waste ends in.

Unfinished in the middle of our field with

snow laying on the ground.

The day is still without a sound.

That is until the chase when the donkeys decided to race.

I opened up the stable door and put their food upon the floor.

I could tell from their demeanour.

They were planning their escape.

And as I rose from the bucket on the floor.

They charged past me and through the door.

Round and round the field they ran dangerously near the tank.

I was fairly large with my seventh child and

worried they would go wild.

My husband was away at the time.

Had he been home all would be fine.

Anyway, I digress let's continue this matter to address.

There I was in my nightgown chasing two donkeys round and round.

Holding on to my belly which at this stage was like a rather large jelly.

Eventually they went back inside to eat their food when they got tired.

They ran me ragged on that day, and I would just love to say.

"I rounded them up and got them inside."

If I had said that I would have lied.

They looked at me as they strolled back in.

With heads cocked to one side.

I am very sure that I saw them grin.

© 2018 Taylor Crowshaw

The Rat Run

Now I am not fond of rats.

Although I am fond of cats.

It is one of those situations.

If you have one you won't have the other.

There are only two variations.

One day when I went out.

I let out an awful shout.

I had gone to feed the chickens.

As I stood looking into the shed at those chickens in their beds.

What do you think I saw weaving in and out of the holes in those old stone walls?

Father, mother and baby rats in a line.

May I say looking quite fine.

On the food I had unwittingly supplied.

They didn't even try to hide.

Now this problem had to be resolved.

Here is how the plan evolved.

My husband decided I would have to clear the shed, and lay poison in their beds.

I went inside the empty shed.

He locked the door behind me.

He stood on the other side.

Shouting orders to me inside.

We managed to get rid of them.

Or should I say.

I did on that day.

We soon got a couple of cats.

Eventually that was that.

No more rats.

© 2018 Taylor Crowshaw

Our Houses

Full of enthusiasm to get started on this house.

We had to clear it out, there had been rats and the odd mouse.

We hid behind our hands.

When we realised our plans.

Had we bitten off more than we could chew.

We'd just have to get on with it what else could we do.

The neighbours must have thought us mad as we pulled up the weeds.

We just saw it as our house and what else did we need.

Derelict houses were our stock in trade.

Many a block stacked and laid.

Windows out windows in doorways out and doorways in.

Walls knocked down what a din.

Ceilings down ceilings up.

"Hey love will you bring me tea.

Make sure it's in my big cup."

Pits filled in and others dug out.

Many arguments when I did scream and shout.

Kids needing attention.

I thought I had better give that a mention.

I don't wish to neglect them it wasn't my intention.

Long cold months of making do. Mud and dust were our companions.

As the Summer came and went.

In the work we made a large dent.

Not too much more to complete.

After which we could rest and put up our feet.

Our life for the last twenty years or so has followed this pattern.

As we get older and slow down.

When we see more work, we tend to frown.

There is many a story to be told of those years.

So, watch this space closely.

You never know I might just tickle your ears.

© 2018 Taylor Crowshaw

Sandgrown

Oh, how happy I would be if I could wander by the sea.

Sandgrown, one of Cods Army that is me.

Meat paste and sand sandwiches on Rossall Beach.

The Floods of 77 wading home knee deep.

I've got myself into a jam.

I wandered off.

I moved away from the fresh sea air.

The problem is.

The real bug bear.

I grew a family elsewhere.

For all of us who miss home.

© 2018 Taylor Crowshaw

Part Four: The Intermission

The Intermission

In the middle of my life.

My mother added to my strife.

A tale of love and warring factions.

A tale of consequences from her actions.

Please read on with open hearts and minds.

Do try not to judge but only to be kind.

Who of us can say with honesty?

Our actions never hurt anyone examine your hearts and see.

The Bible tells us that the truth will set us free,

and the old saying "What will be will be."

Both of these are true but sometimes the truth is brandished like a sword.

Used for harm and not to heal.

Judge for yourself when the truth I reveal.

© 2018 Taylor Crowshaw

Mum's Stalker

Now this is how it did unfold.

A short tale which needs to be told.

After years it has become clear.

We should have known there was something wrong here.

Arriving home from school one day.

I could hear quite an affray.

Aunty June sat in a chair.

Mother shouting and pointing at her.

When they realised I was there, they became quiet.

I didn't know what was wrong I just thought it a riot.

Aunty ceased her sarcastic quips.

As mother raised her fingers to her lips.

Everywhere we went that year.

Aunty June would appear.

It all came to a head.

One night whilst we were in bed.

My dad's brother banged at the door.

We all ran across the floor.

Out of the window we could see dad and his brother arms a flailing.

Aunty and mother shouting and wailing.

After a while my uncle drove off my father helped him on his way.

It was years before we even spoke about that day.

My mother told us aunty had suspected her affair.

That on that night she had made my uncle aware.

I often wonder if my father knew.

That we might not be his children, was he aware?

I cannot even ask him, now that he is gone.

Would I even do that, would I be that one?

Many years have passed by.

Sometimes I ask myself why.

She never told us until my dad had died.

Even if she had I would not have asked him.

No, I would not have been that one.

© 2018 Taylor Crowshaw

Dads Demise

One year on my mum was over.

Helping us paint she was like a pig in clover.

She brought my second son for a visit.

He had moved back home to be with his father.

Whilst here mum got a call.

My father he had had a fall.

He lay all night on the floor.

Until my son called at the door.

They travelled home hand in hand.

Trying hard to understand.

What had gone wrong no way to know.

Until they reached home they had to let it go.

My dad had had a massive stroke.

Later on, as my sister spoke.

My mother's resolve finally broke.

In tears she sat by his bed, but hers were not the only tears shed.

He never fully recovered from that night.

He lay in bed most of the time, he had lost his fight.

My mother nursed him at home for four long years.

My eldest son at her right side to help her out and wipe her tears.

His wife, his son, grandsons, and daughter.

Sat by his bed that day.

As my father passed away.

A phone call was how I found out.

We had no phone my neighbour called.

I cradled my daughter just five weeks old.

I rocked and cried as I was told.

The last words he ever said to me.

"If you hadn't moved away, I wouldn't be lying here today."

© 2018 Taylor Crowshaw

To Be Offered Up A Dad

Still grieving for our beloved dad.

We were delighted that October.

When mum decided to come over.

She brought a friend from years before.

A lover who had long ago walked out the door.

His wife was my mums best friend.

But not always and not to the end.

We had lost our dad that June.

To get such news it was too soon.

Mum said she had something to tell us.

I joked and said, "You're not going to tell us he is our dad."

The joke was on me he was that very lad.

She said that dad was not our dad.

That it was this other lad.

We had a test, DNA doesn't lie.

I could not deny it and would not try.

We were devastated to realise.

Our young lives were based on lies.

He was a kind man in many ways.

All he wanted was his old lover.

Not to bond with children he never knew.

Mum thought it would unite us all.

It was too much of a call.

Two years on mum got ill.

No cure for her no magic pill.

He nursed and loved her for the rest of her life.

She never realised her wish to become his wife.

Enough love shared in their six years.

Making up for mum's unhappy years.

After just one short year he became ill too.

We all tried to cheer him on.

All he wanted was to be gone.

He'd lost his love, his life.

After all was said and done my father never was supplanted.

© 2018 Taylor Crowshaw

Conception

My sister and I had many questions.

One of which regarded our conception.

We also needed to know if our original dad was indeed my brother's dad.

She said that he was his dad and not this other lad.

Did this other man's family know?

She said they did.

At times it is where they would go.

With his sister they would stay.

On their occasional trips away.

So many questions to ask.

Mother stayed behind her mask.

She thought it so romantic.

To us it all seemed frantic.

Meeting here and there.

A brief moment to share.

Furtive glances. Taking chances.

Hard to hear and hard to bear.

Our start in life of which we were made aware.

Hard to believe this man did not know of our young lives with so much strife.

But then he had another family and a wife.

© 2018 Taylor Crowshaw

The Name Change

You may have noticed that my name fluctuates.

Between certain times and dates.

There is a good reason why and

there is no point my being shy.

When I found out my dad was not my dad, and that it was this other lad.

It was a time of great confusion,

realising my life had been an illusion.

As I have said before I was fond of my father who had been in waiting.

I needed something to connect to him.

I didn't do this name change on a whim.

They say its nature not nurture how we turn out.

When I found out this other man loved all things the same as me.

Animals, music, and even wrote poetry.

He always had madcap schemes.

These are the things of my dreams.

So, one day I decided that I would change

my name.

At work the girls and I treated it like a game.

They would walk around.

Trying each day, a different name to see how it would sound.

I went back home to see my new dad.

I told him of the plans I had.

To change my Christian name, and instead use his surname.

I sat at his side with my youngest child on my knee.

On his other side stood his oxygen tank.

All he did was look at me.

Just as I was about to rise, a teardrop

trickled from his eye.

He sighed, and with a shaky voice he said to me,

"Do you know love you're the only one who

can make me cry."

My daughter made me a name badge for work.

Which I pinned onto my shirt.

When my workmates did forget.

I would point to my chest.

Whereupon that badge did rest.

Although at times I feel sad about my youth.

My new name reminds me of the truth.

© 2018 Taylor Crowshaw

A Father in Waiting

To us it was devastating.

To have a father in waiting.

Growing up with my dad.

Boy oh boy what a lad.

We got to our forties don't you know.

Was it all just for show?

My dad's my dad no looking back.

Sometimes it's better not to know.

Just to maintain the status quo.

© 2018 Taylor Crowshaw

Conclusion: Words

Words

It is a fact indeed, that as soon as I learnt how to read.

Upon those precious words I'd feed.

There is no point in being pretentious.

Let's just say it was an eclectic mix, on which I would get my fix.

Literature in our house was in short supply.

I didn't let that stop me and you will find out why.

Whilst I ate my breakfast I would read the cereal packet.

Saxa Salt was fascinating, and vinegar was thrilling.

My mother's latest book was probably quite chilling.

Charles Dickens, Dennis Wheatley, Harold Robbins, The Bronte sisters, all kept me addicted.

You may think for one so young some of those authors were quite wrong.

Just between me and you.

Those were the only words that I had access to.

Out of all of that was born.

An imagination a love of words, and of creation.

This poem is not the end of my story.

I am sure that you can tell, but you will have to wait for the rest until the words

compel.

© 2018 Taylor Crowshaw

This last poem is an ode to my daughter's Great Dane Albert, whose untimely death started me on this journey.

Albert

When first I picked you out, you were so small and cute.

Who knew you would grow up so handsome in your jet-black evening suite.

Calum, Shay and Tasha, your friends your family.

They were all you ever wanted, and where you wanted to be.

Sometimes you were powerful as mighty as a bear.

Or nimble as a ballerina spinning the air.

From the corner of my eye I would see you ears pricked and ready.

As I rode my horse, keeping him on course taking it steady.

I can even smell you now my goodness your farts were smelly,

But as I think of you my knees turn into jelly.

No more that rumble in your belly turning into a bellow.

Goodbye old chap goodbye old friend you were a lovely fellow.

Albert

2010 – 2017

© 2018 Taylor Crowshaw

Part Five: Perpetual Motion

I have included the following poems in my book in acknowledgement of the wonderful, and evocative content. Written by two talented poets, musicians, and artists, my sons.

Perpetual Motion

I am the book keeper,

the ultimate accumulator.

I am the voice of energy

I am your hearts generator.

I eat with your eyes.

When you sleep I will rise,

but the laws will prevail

and surely, I will die.

Looking to save the universe.

Planting machines that multiplied,

Recreating each other.

Thermodynamics,

The second law applies

I am a contribution.

Forever is no lie.

Like everything that exists,

I will shrivel as I die

The law becomes the reason,

no matter what we try.

Reference: Golden Calibre Copyright 2018

SPIRIT

All information based into one mind.

All separate people.

Each one of a kind.

Everything we see, everything I do.

Everything that happens,

Happens for you.

Am I on my own?

Am I you alone?

Will my roots from under me,

Bring an end to my misery.

Now I'm lost in the distance.

I have multiplied.

Somewhere in the middle.

At least this way I can hide.

Now I look down upon my papers.

Now I look into the sky.

Where is my life's creator?

This world has left me behind.

I long to know my purpose.

I pine for a return

Somewhere in time I'll find ourselves.

And my brother's and loves I will learn.

Reference: Golden Calibre Copyright 2018

Part Six: Tomorrow

Tomorrow

Stepping out into the sun

blue skies and warm

feeling like there is a future

a battle that could be won

but doubt creeps

as my worries sleep

tomorrow is drawing close

I stumble on thought

hope the ever-burning flame

mind cast into the future

wondering if things will turn out

positive

negative

intermediate

travelling from A to Z

can't stop to breathe

to see.

I am blind.

© 2018 Daemon Cantrell

Strawberry Letter 24

I was flying on a rainbows stream

floating in a perfumed dream.

In the message I could not do more

strawberry letter twenty-four.

Smooth diamonds flow from your tongue

roses with no thorns cannot be wrong.

I dance and shimmer through the snow

pure white and blue only you would know.

Wrap yourself in satins hands again

keep wrapped happy and warm.

I will be there with you in thought

to cradle you till the dawn.

When you wake I'll be back with you

and our hearts will beat in two.

From bass to body and sound

our music brings us round.

So until we meet again

let our minds intertwine

to think as one

as one mind.

© 2018 Daemon Cantrell

Born in Lancashire in 1959.

Mother to ten wonderful children, grandmother to nineteen and great grandmother to one.

I live on a smallholding in Ireland with my husband Peter and youngest daughter, Fleur, four dogs, two cats, five donkeys and numerous chickens.

Thank you for reading and look out for the next book of poems, a lighthearted look at growing older.

12523880R00058

Printed in Great Britain
by Amazon